GLP-1 Diet Cookbook for Beginners

90-Day Meal Plan with 5-Ingredient Recipes to Boost Weight Loss, Curb Cravings, and Support Energy for Users of Medications Like Ozempic, Wegovy & Mounjaro.

Abigail Douglas

Table of Contents

GLP-1 Diet Cookbook for Beginners 1

Preface 13

Introduction 17

    How to Use This Book 20

Chapter 1 24

    Understanding the GLP-1 Diet Lifestyle 24

        What GLP-1 Medications Do — In Plain Language 25

        Why Diet Still Matters — Even When You're Not Hungry 26

        Balancing Protein, Fiber, and Healthy Fats for Energy 27

Common Mistakes People Make — and How to Avoid Them 29

Chapter 2 32

Preparing for Your 90-Day Journey 32

Setting Realistic Expectations for the Next 3 Months 32

Managing Appetite Changes and Side Effects 34

Creating a Supportive Kitchen Environment 35

Grocery Shopping Strategies for 5-Ingredient Cooking 36

Chapter 3 39

Your GLP-1 Friendly Pantry 39

Must-Have Staples for Quick, Easy, and Nutrient-Dense Meals 39

Proteins (Shelf, Fridge, and Freezer) 40

Whole Grains & Carb Sources 41

Healthy Fats 42

Vegetables (Fresh & Frozen) 42

Low-Calorie, High-Protein Snacks That Won't Upset the Stomach 42

Foods to Limit for Better Tolerance 44

Chapter 4 47

90-Day Meal Plan Overview 47

How the Plan is Structured — 3 Phases for Success

.... 47

Portion Guidance for Reduced Appetite 50

Weekly Rotation Themes to Prevent Boredom 51

Chapter 5 53

Phase 1 (Days 1–30) – Reset & Nourish 53

Why This Phase Matters 54

5 Strategies for Easing into the GLP-1 Lifestyle 54

5-Ingredient Breakfast Ideas 56

1. Greek Yogurt Berry Bowl 56

2. Spinach & Egg Scramble 56

3. Banana Almond Smoothie 57

5-Ingredient Lunch Ideas 58

1. Turkey & Avocado Wrap..58

2. Quinoa Chickpea Salad..58

5-Ingredient Dinner Ideas 59

1. Lemon Herb Salmon 59

2. Chicken & Veggie Stir-Fry 59

5-Ingredient Snack Ideas...60

1. Cottage Cheese & Pineapple..60

2. Roasted Almonds 61

Phase 1 Daily Structure Example 61

Chapter 6 63

Phase 2 (Days 31–60) – Boost & Balance..................63

Increasing Variety While Keeping Simplicity 64

Introducing Mild Spice, New Proteins, and Fiber-Rich Sides 65

   Protein Upgrades: 65

   Fiber-Rich Side Ideas: 66

Handling Cravings Without Sabotaging Progress 66

5-Ingredient Recipe Ideas for Phase 2 67

   Breakfast: Spiced Veggie Omelet 67

   Lunch: Shrimp & Quinoa Salad 68

   Dinner: Turkey & Sweet Potato Tray Bake 68

   Snack: Cinnamon Yogurt Dip with Apple Slices ... 69

Chapter 7 71

Phase 3 (Days 61–90) – Sustain & Thrive 71

Building Habits for Long-Term Maintenance 72

How to Reintroduce Certain Foods Carefully 73

Planning Meals for Travel, Work, and Social Events 74

5-Ingredient Meal Ideas for Phase 3 76

    Breakfast: Veggie & Feta Egg Muffins................. 76

    Lunch: Grilled Chicken & Lentil Salad................. 76

    Dinner: Baked Cod with Zucchini Noodles........... 77

Chapter 8 79

    Side Effect Solutions in the Kitchen........................... 79

    Meal Adjustments for Nausea...................................... 79

        Tips for Cooking Through Nausea:........................ 80

        GLP-1-Friendly Recipe Ideas for Nausea:.............. 80

Meal Adjustments for Constipation 81

Tips for Beating Constipation: 81

GLP-1-Friendly Recipe Ideas for Constipation: 82

Meal Adjustments for Low Appetite 83

Tips for Boosting Nutrient Intake in Small Portions: 83

GLP-1-Friendly Recipe Ideas for Low Appetite: .. 83

Comfort Foods That Still Align with Goals 84

Hydration Tips and Soothing Snacks 85

Chapter 9 88

5-Ingredient Recipe Collection 88

BREAKFAST (15 Recipes) 89

LUNCH (15 Recipes) 91

DINNER (20 Recipes) 93

SNACKS (15 Recipes) 95

Chapter 10 98

Mindset & Motivation for Lasting Change 98

Why Motivation Alone Isn't Enough 99

Creating Food Freedom Without Sabotaging Results 99

Celebrating Small Wins 100

Tracking Progress Beyond the Scale 101

Chapter 11 103

Beyond the 90 Days – Your Long-Term GLP-1 Lifestyle 103

Adapting Meal Plans After Medication Changes 104

Transitioning to Intuitive Eating While Keeping Results 104

Using Your New Skills for Lifelong Wellness 105

Your Next Steps 106

Glossary of Terms 108

Acknowledgments 113

Copyright © 2025 by Abigail Douglas

All rights reserved. No part of this book may be copied, reproduced, stored, or transmitted in any form or by any means—electronic, mechanical, photocopying, recording, or otherwise without prior written permission from the publisher, except for brief quotations used in reviews or scholarly works.

DISCLAIMER

This book is intended for informational and educational purposes only. It is not intended to diagnose, treat, cure, or prevent any medical condition. The recipes, meal plans, and lifestyle suggestions provided are based on general nutrition principles and are not a substitute for professional medical advice.

Always consult with your physician, dietitian, or qualified healthcare provider before making any changes to your diet, medication, or exercise routine, especially if you are currently taking GLP-1 medications such as Ozempic, Wegovy, or Mounjaro. Individual results may vary, and any dietary changes should be tailored to your personal health needs. The author and publisher disclaim any liability arising directly or indirectly from the use of the information contained in this book.

Preface

Over the past few years, GLP-1 medications like **Ozempic**, **Wegovy**, and **Mounjaro** have completely transformed the weight loss conversation. For millions, they've offered something long thought impossible — a way to finally gain control over hunger, improve blood sugar management, and make lasting progress toward a healthier body.

But here's the truth I've seen again and again: the medication is only half the story. To truly thrive on a GLP-1 journey — whether your goal is weight loss, appetite control, or improved energy — you need a way of eating that works with your body, not against it. And that's exactly why I created this book.

The GLP-1 Diet Cookbook for Beginners is your go-to companion for turning the appetite-suppressing benefits of GLP-1 therapy into a real-life, sustainable lifestyle. This isn't a restrictive diet or a one-size-fits-all plan. Instead, it's a 90-day roadmap packed with:

- 5-ingredient recipes that are quick, flavorful, and gentle on digestion.
- A structured meal plan designed specifically for reduced appetite while meeting your nutritional needs.
- Practical tips for managing side effects like nausea, constipation, and low appetite without derailing your progress.
- Tools to help you eat well at home, at work, while traveling, or at social events.
- Guidance for transitioning to intuitive eating and keeping results for life.

I've filled this book with GLP-1-friendly breakfasts, lunches, dinners, and snacks that are high in protein, rich in fiber, and balanced with healthy fats. Every meal is designed to fuel your body on fewer calories without sacrificing taste or satisfaction. And because I know variety is key, you'll find weekly rotation themes, customizable swaps for vegetarian and dairy-free diets, and make-ahead options for busy days.

Whether you're brand new to GLP-1 medications or looking for a way to maintain your weight loss results, this book is here to guide you from your very first meal to your long-term lifestyle.

My hope is that as you work through the Reset & Nourish, Boost & Balance, and Sustain & Thrive phases, you'll not only see physical changes but also feel empowered to make confident food choices — long after the 90 days are over.

Your journey toward a healthier, more energized, and more balanced life starts here. And I promise — it's going to be simpler, more delicious, and more sustainable than you think.

Introduction

If you've picked up this book, chances are you're ready to take control of your health, reshape your relationship with food, and get the very best results from your GLP-1 journey. Whether you're using medications like **Ozempic**, **Wegovy**, or **Mounjaro**, or you're simply following a **GLP-1 diet plan** to support weight loss and better energy, you're in the right place.

Over the past few years, GLP-1 therapies have transformed the weight loss landscape. They work by helping curb cravings, slow digestion, and keep you feeling full longer — giving your body a powerful reset. But here's the truth: **what you eat still matters**. Choosing the right foods can mean the difference between simply losing a few pounds and building a healthier, sustainable lifestyle you actually enjoy. That's where this book comes in.

The **GLP-1 Diet Cookbook for Beginners** is designed to be your everyday guide — a trusted companion with **easy 5-ingredient recipes**, a **structured 90-day meal plan**, and **practical tips** to keep you energized, satisfied, and moving toward your goals. Every meal in this book has been created with GLP-1 users in mind, focusing on high-protein, nutrient-dense, and gentle-on-the-stomach ingredients that work with your body, not against it.

Inside these pages, you'll find:

- **Fast, no-fuss meals** ready in 20 minutes or less.
- **Simple meal plans** that take the guesswork out of eating.
- **GLP-1-friendly snacks and comfort foods** to support weight loss without feeling deprived.
- **Real-life tips** for managing side effects like nausea, low appetite, or food fatigue.

- **Smart grocery shopping strategies** so your kitchen is always stocked with the essentials.

This isn't just another diet book. It's a **practical, sustainable guide** that fits real life — whether you're cooking for yourself, your family, or on the go. You don't need to be a gourmet chef or spend hours in the kitchen. All you need is a handful of ingredients, a few minutes of your day, and the willingness to invest in yourself.

Your **GLP-1 weight loss journey** doesn't have to feel restrictive or complicated. With the right approach, it can be delicious, energizing, and surprisingly simple. By the end of these 90 days, you'll not only feel lighter and more confident, but you'll also have the skills and habits to maintain your results for the long haul.

So, grab your grocery list, open your mind to new flavors, and let's make your GLP-1 diet a fresh start that sticks — one easy, nourishing meal at a time.

How to Use This Book

Starting a new eating plan can feel overwhelming — especially when your appetite, cravings, and energy levels are shifting with GLP-1 therapy. This book is designed to take the stress out of the process and replace it with clarity, structure, and flavor. Here's how to make the most of it.

1. Start With the Basics

Before diving into the meal plan, read through Chapter 1 to understand how the GLP-1 diet works, why certain foods support your journey better than others, and how to manage common challenges like nausea or reduced appetite.

2. Stock Your GLP-1-Friendly Kitchen

Head to Chapter 3 to set up your pantry and fridge with the essentials. Keeping a few core ingredients on hand will make sticking to the plan effortless, even on busy days.

3. Follow the 90-Day Meal Plan — or Mix and Match

In Chapters 4–7, you'll find a structured, easy-to-follow plan broken into three phases: Reset & Nourish, Boost & Balance, and Sustain & Thrive.

If you love structure, follow the plan exactly as written.

If you prefer flexibility, mix and match recipes from Chapter 9 using the portion guidance provided.

4. Keep It Simple With 5 Ingredients

Every recipe in this book uses five core ingredients or fewer (plus pantry staples like salt, pepper, or olive oil). This makes cooking fast, affordable, and less overwhelming — perfect for busy schedules and smaller appetites.

5. Listen to Your Body

GLP-1 medications can change how your body responds to food. You may feel full faster or crave different flavors. Use the recipes and tips as a guide, but don't force yourself to eat more than you're comfortable with.

6. Lean on the Side Effect Solutions

If you experience discomfort, Chapter 8 offers gentle, nourishing recipes and hydration strategies to help you feel better without derailing your progress.

7. Track Your Wins

Use the printable 90-Day Meal Planner & Shopping List included at the back of the book (or download the bonus version online) to plan ahead, track your meals, and celebrate every milestone — big or small.

8. Keep the Lifestyle Going

Once you complete the 90 days, Chapter 11 will guide you on how to adapt your plan for long-term success, whether you stay on medication or not.

This is more than a cookbook — it's a companion for your weight loss journey. Take it one meal, one day, and one week at a time. The goal isn't perfection; it's progress you can feel proud of.

Chapter 1

Understanding the GLP-1 Diet Lifestyle

If you're reading this, chances are you've either just started taking a GLP-1 medication like **Ozempic**, **Wegovy**, or **Mounjaro** — or you're considering it. Maybe you've already noticed your appetite shrinking. Maybe you feel full faster, or you're skipping meals without even realizing it.

At first, this can feel like magic. But here's the truth: **the key to lasting weight loss and better health isn't just what these medications do — it's what you do alongside them.**

This chapter will help you understand exactly how GLP-1 medications work in plain language, why your diet still matters even when you're not as hungry, and how to balance your plate to feel good and stay energized. You'll also learn the most common mistakes people make and how you can avoid them from day one.

What GLP-1 Medications Do — In Plain Language

GLP-1 stands for **Glucagon-Like Peptide-1**, a natural hormone your body releases when you eat. Its job is to:

- Help control blood sugar after meals.
- Slow down how fast food leaves your stomach.
- Send "I'm full" signals to your brain.

When you take a GLP-1 medication, you're essentially giving your body an extra dose of this fullness signal. That means:

- You feel satisfied with less food.

- You crave snacks and sweets less often.
- You have fewer energy crashes after meals.

Think of it as having a built-in "pause" button between bites — giving your brain time to recognize that you've eaten enough.

But here's the important part: GLP-1 medications **don't choose your meals for you**. They make it easier to eat less, but you still have to decide what goes on your plate.

Why Diet Still Matters — Even When You're Not Hungry

Some people think, *If I'm eating less, I can eat whatever I want and still lose weight*. In the short term, this might seem true. But long term, it can backfire.

Here's why:

- **Nutrient gaps** — Eating tiny portions of low-quality food can leave you tired, cranky, and nutrient-deficient.
- **Muscle loss** — Without enough protein, your body may burn muscle along with fat.
- **Energy dips** — Skipping balanced meals can lead to sluggishness and brain fog.

The GLP-1 diet lifestyle is about **making the most of each bite**. Since you're eating less overall, every meal is an opportunity to give your body the protein, fiber, vitamins, and healthy fats it needs to stay strong.

Balancing Protein, Fiber, and Healthy Fats for Energy

Think of your meals as a simple triangle — each side representing one of your three key building blocks:

1. **Protein** – Keeps you full longer, preserves lean muscle, and supports a steady metabolism.

- Examples: eggs, chicken breast, Greek yogurt, tofu, fish.

2. **Fiber** – Helps digestion, supports gut health, and keeps blood sugar steady.

- Examples: leafy greens, berries, beans, chia seeds.

3. **Healthy fats** – Support brain function, hormone balance, and satisfaction after meals.

- Examples: avocado, olive oil, nuts, seeds.

If your plate consistently has all three, you'll feel energized without the spikes and crashes that come from carb-heavy or processed meals.

Quick tip: When in doubt, build a plate that's half vegetables, a quarter protein, and a quarter healthy carbs (like quinoa or sweet potato), topped with a drizzle of healthy fat.

Common Mistakes People Make — and How to Avoid Them

Mistake 1: Skipping too many meals

When you're not hungry, it's tempting to go without eating for hours. But if you regularly skip meals, you may end up undernourished and more likely to overeat later.

Fix: Eat small, balanced meals every 3–4 hours, even if they're lighter than before.

Mistake 2: Relying on processed "diet foods"

Low-calorie snacks, frozen diet dinners, and sugar-free treats might seem convenient, but they often lack real nutrition.

Fix: Focus on whole, minimally processed foods with natural nutrients.

Mistake 3: Forgetting hydration

GLP-1 medications can sometimes make people forget to drink water — leading to headaches, constipation, or fatigue.

Fix: Keep a water bottle nearby and aim for at least 6–8 cups a day.

Mistake 4: Not getting enough protein

Without adequate protein, you risk losing muscle instead of just fat.

Fix: Include protein in every meal — even snacks.

The Takeaway:

GLP-1 medications can be a powerful tool for weight loss and appetite control, but they work best when paired with intentional, balanced eating. By focusing on nutrient-rich foods and avoiding common pitfalls, you set yourself up for not just weight loss, but better health, more energy, and sustainable habits that last well beyond the medication.

Chapter 2

Preparing for Your 90-Day Journey

Starting your 90-day GLP-1 diet journey is more than just following a meal plan — it's about creating the right mindset, environment, and habits to make success feel natural, not forced. Whether you're here to lose weight, boost your energy, or simply feel better in your own skin, the next three months will be about building small, sustainable changes that add up to big results.

Setting Realistic Expectations for the Next 3 Months

It's tempting to hope for dramatic transformations overnight, especially when you're using a GLP-1 medication like **Ozempic**, **Wegovy**, or **Mounjaro**. And yes — these medications can help reduce appetite and cravings quickly. But lasting success comes when you focus on more than just the number on the scale.

Here's what realistic progress can look like:

- **Steady, sustainable weight loss** — Think 1–2 pounds per week, sometimes more in the first month.
- **Better control over cravings** — You may notice certain snacks or late-night eating habits fade naturally.
- **Increased energy and focus** — When your meals are balanced, your body will run more efficiently.
- **More confidence in the kitchen** — As you practice quick, healthy cooking, it will become second nature.

Remember: every small step forward is a win. A slow, steady pace is not only healthier, it's more likely to stick for the long term.

Managing Appetite Changes and Side Effects

One of the most noticeable changes you'll experience on GLP-1 therapy is reduced appetite. This can be both a blessing and a challenge. Eating less can help you lose weight, but if you eat too little or skip meals too often, you risk missing important nutrients.

Tips for Managing Appetite Changes:

- Eat smaller, nutrient-dense meals every 3–4 hours.
- Prioritize protein first, then add fiber-rich vegetables, and healthy fats.
- Keep healthy snacks like Greek yogurt, boiled eggs, or sliced cucumber within easy reach.

Handling Common Side Effects:

- Nausea – Choose light, easy-to-digest foods like soups, smoothies, or steamed vegetables.

- Constipation – Increase your fiber gradually and drink plenty of water.
- Low energy – Make sure you're getting enough protein and complex carbs like quinoa or sweet potato.

***Pro Tip:** Your appetite may fluctuate from week to week. Listen to your body — some days you may need more food, other days less. That's perfectly normal.*

Creating a Supportive Kitchen Environment

Your environment can make or break your success. If your fridge and pantry are stocked with the right foods, you'll find it much easier to stick to the plan — even on busy or stressful days.

Steps to Create a Supportive Kitchen:

1. Clear out trigger foods — If it tempts you but doesn't serve your goals, donate or store it out of sight.

2. Designate a "GLP-1 Shelf" — Keep your go-to proteins, veggies, and snacks in one easy-to-reach spot.

3. Invest in a few basics — A sharp knife, a non-stick skillet, and airtight containers will make meal prep fast and painless.

Grocery Shopping Strategies for 5-Ingredient Cooking

One of the biggest benefits of this cookbook is its 5-ingredient recipes. Not only do they save time, they make healthy eating more affordable and less overwhelming.

Here's how to shop smart:

- **Make a master list** — Write down the proteins, vegetables, whole grains, and healthy fats you use most often.

- **Buy in bulk where it makes sense** — Chicken breast, salmon, eggs, quinoa, and frozen vegetables store well.
- **Choose versatile ingredients** — Spinach can be used in omelets, salads, and smoothies; quinoa works as a base for both savory and sweet bowls.
- **Shop the perimeter** — Most fresh, whole foods are along the outer aisles of the grocery store.

Example Weekly Shopping List:

- Proteins: chicken breast, salmon, eggs, Greek yogurt
- Vegetables: broccoli, bell peppers, spinach, cherry tomatoes
- Whole grains: quinoa, brown rice
- Healthy fats: avocado, olive oil, almonds

The Takeaway:

Preparing for your 90-day journey is about setting yourself

up for success before you even cook your first meal. By having the right expectations, understanding how to manage changes in appetite, and stocking your kitchen with the right foods, you make it far easier to follow through and much more enjoyable.

Chapter 3

Your GLP-1 Friendly Pantry

If your kitchen is stocked with the right foods, healthy eating becomes almost automatic. On busy days, when you don't feel like cooking or your appetite is low, having a GLP-1-friendly pantry means you can pull together a quick, nourishing meal in minutes — without falling back on processed or nutrient-poor options.

This chapter is your blueprint for creating a pantry, fridge, and freezer that work with your goals. You'll learn which staples to keep on hand, the best low-calorie, high-protein snacks for when hunger strikes, and which foods to limit for better comfort and tolerance while on GLP-1 therapy.

Must-Have Staples for Quick, Easy, and Nutrient-

Dense Meals

Think of your pantry as your personal meal-building station. Everything here should help you prepare simple, balanced dishes with minimal effort. Since this cookbook focuses on 5-ingredient recipes, these staples are versatile enough to be used in multiple meals.

Proteins (Shelf, Fridge, and Freezer)

- **Canned tuna or salmon** – Quick for salads or wraps.
- **Eggs** – Perfect for breakfasts, snacks, or quick dinners.
- **Chicken breast (fresh or frozen)** – Lean, versatile, and easy to season.

- **Greek yogurt (plain, unsweetened)** – A protein-rich base for breakfast or snacks.
- **Tofu or tempeh** – Great plant-based options for variety.

Whole Grains & Carb Sources

- **Quinoa** – High in protein and fiber; cooks in under 20 minutes.
- **Brown rice** – Pairs with almost any protein or vegetable.
- **Oats** – Great for breakfast bowls or blending into smoothies.
- **Whole grain wraps or tortillas** – For quick lunches or dinner roll-ups.

Healthy Fats

- **Avocados** – Healthy, creamy, and filling.
- **Olive oil** – Heart-healthy and perfect for cooking or salads.
- **Nuts and seeds** – Almonds, chia seeds, and pumpkin seeds for crunch and nutrients.

Vegetables (Fresh & Frozen)

- **Spinach or kale** – Quick to sauté or blend into smoothies.
- **Bell peppers** – Colorful, crunchy, and vitamin-rich.
- **Broccoli** – High in fiber and vitamin C.
- **Frozen mixed vegetables** – A fast side dish or soup add-in.

Low-Calorie, High-Protein Snacks

That Won't Upset the Stomach

GLP-1 medications can make large snacks feel uncomfortable, so aim for light but nutrient-dense options. These keep you full without overwhelming your appetite or digestion.

- **Hard-boiled eggs** – Easy to prepare in batches.
- **Low-fat cheese sticks** – Portable and portion-controlled.
- **Turkey or chicken slices** – Roll with lettuce for a quick snack wrap.
- **Protein smoothies** – Blend protein powder with almond milk and berries.
- **Cottage cheese** – Light, creamy, and versatile.
- **Roasted chickpeas** – Crunchy, high-protein alternative to chips.

Tip: Keep snacks pre-portioned in small containers so you can grab them quickly without overeating.

Foods to Limit for Better Tolerance

While GLP-1 medications don't come with a one-size-fits-all food restriction list, some foods can cause discomfort — especially in the early weeks.

- **Greasy or fried foods** – These can worsen nausea or slow digestion even more.
- **Sugary drinks** – They can spike blood sugar and cause energy crashes.
- **Highly processed snacks** – Chips, candy, and pastries offer little nutrition and can lead to stomach upset.
- **Carbonated beverages** – May cause bloating or discomfort.
- **Very spicy foods** – Some people find they trigger acid reflux.

Pro Tip: *Instead of cutting out favorites forever, try* *smaller portions or gentler cooking methods (baking instead of frying, lightly seasoning instead of heavily spicing).*

The Takeaway:

A GLP-1-friendly pantry is about simplicity and support. When your kitchen is filled with high-quality staples, you won't waste time wondering what to eat — you'll have the building blocks for quick, healthy meals at your fingertips.

Chapter 4

90-Day Meal Plan Overview

You're about to begin a 90-day journey designed to help you **lose weight, boost energy,** and **build a sustainable eating routine** — all while working with your body's changing appetite on GLP-1 therapy. This is not a rigid, one-size-fits-all diet. It's a structured yet flexible plan that adapts to your needs, preferences, and daily life.

By following this guide, **you'll know exactly what to eat, when to eat, and how to prepare it** — without spending hours in the kitchen or feeling deprived.

How the Plan is Structured — 3 Phases for Success

The 90 days are broken into **three manageable** phases.

Each phase lasts 30 days and builds on the one before it, gradually increasing variety and flavor while reinforcing healthy habits.

Phase 1 – Reset & Nourish (Days 1–30)

This is your gentle start. You'll focus on easy-to-digest, nutrient-rich meals that are light but satisfying. The recipes here are simple, mild in flavor, and designed to help you adjust to appetite changes.

Key Goals:

- Reduce processed foods and added sugars.
- Focus on lean protein, fresh vegetables, and whole grains.
- Stabilize energy levels and digestion.

Phase 2 – Boost & Balance (Days 31–60)

Now that your body is used to smaller, balanced meals, we'll introduce more variety and flavor. You'll experiment with new seasonings, colorful produce, and a wider range of protein sources.

Key Goals:

- Keep meals interesting to avoid food fatigue.
- Increase fiber for better digestion.
- Continue meeting protein needs to preserve muscle.

Phase 3 – Sustain & Thrive (Days 61–90)

In this phase, you'll focus on building long-term habits. Recipes will include more diverse cooking methods and meal options for dining out, traveling, and social events.

Key Goals:

- Transition into a sustainable lifestyle beyond 90 days.
- Learn how to adapt recipes for different situations.
- Develop confidence in creating balanced meals without relying on the plan.

Portion Guidance for Reduced Appetite

One of the most important adjustments on GLP-1 therapy is learning how to eat enough for nourishment without overeating.

General Guidelines:

- **Protein first:** Aim for 2–4 ounces per meal (about the size of your palm).
- **Vegetables second:** Fill about half your plate with non-starchy vegetables.
- **Healthy carbs:** Choose small portions (½ cup cooked quinoa, sweet potato, or brown rice).
- **Healthy fats:** Add 1–2 teaspoons of olive oil, avocado, or nuts for flavor and satisfaction.

Tip: If you feel full halfway through your meal, save the rest for later — listen to your body's cues rather than pushing to finish.

Weekly Rotation Themes to Prevent Boredom

To keep meals fresh and exciting, the plan uses weekly rotation themes. This approach helps you try new flavors without feeling overwhelmed by too much variety at once.

Sample Weekly Themes:

- **Week 1** – Comfort Classics, Lightened Up (soups, stews, oven-baked favorites)
- **Week 2** – Mediterranean Fresh (olive oil, fresh herbs, grilled proteins)
- **Week 3** – Asian-Inspired Simplicity (stir-fries, miso soup, ginger-based marinades)
- **Week 4** – Plant-Powered Focus (hearty vegetarian and vegan dishes)

The themes repeat with new recipes and seasonal ingredients so you'll never get bored — but you'll also never feel like you're starting over from scratch.

The Takeaway:

This 90-day plan gives you structure without rigidity, variety without confusion, and guidance without overwhelm. By the end of three months, you'll have a toolkit of simple recipes, portion awareness, and flavor ideas you can use for life.

Chapter 5

Phase 1 (Days 1–30) – Reset & Nourish

Welcome to your first month on the **GLP-1 diet plan**. This is the Reset & Nourish phase — a gentle introduction that helps your body adjust to appetite changes while giving you all the nutrition you need to feel strong, steady, and satisfied.

Think of this as a soft landing: no overwhelming recipes, no drastic changes overnight. Instead, you'll focus on **simple, easy-to-digest meals** made with **five core ingredients or fewer**. These recipes are designed to work with your reduced appetite, minimize discomfort, and set the stage for long-term success.

Why This Phase Matters

Many people start GLP-1 therapy expecting instant transformation — and while appetite suppression often comes quickly, your body still needs time to adapt. This first month is about:

- **Preventing nutrient gaps** despite smaller meals.
- **Avoiding digestive discomfort** by choosing lighter, well-balanced foods.
- **Building habits** you can carry into the next phases without feeling deprived.

5 Strategies for Easing into the GLP-1 Lifestyle

1. Start Small, Eat Often

Instead of three large meals, try 4–5 smaller, balanced ones. This keeps your energy steady without overloading your stomach.

2. Prioritize Protein

Every meal should have a lean protein source — chicken, eggs, fish, Greek yogurt, or tofu — to help preserve muscle and keep you full.

3. Hydrate Consistently

Thirst can be mistaken for hunger, and dehydration can worsen side effects like constipation. Aim for 6–8 cups of water daily.

4. Listen to Your Body

Stop eating when you're comfortably full, even if that means saving half your meal for later.

5. Keep it Simple

The less you complicate your meals, the easier it will be to stay consistent.

5-Ingredient Breakfast Ideas

Each of these breakfasts is GLP-1 friendly, easy to prepare, and gentle on digestion.

1. Greek Yogurt Berry Bowl

- 1 cup plain Greek yogurt
- ½ cup blueberries
- ½ cup sliced strawberries
- 1 tsp chia seeds
- 1 tsp honey (optional)

Why it works: High-protein, antioxidant-rich, and light on the stomach.

2. Spinach & Egg Scramble

- 2 eggs

- 1 cup baby spinach
- 1 tbsp olive oil
- Salt & pepper
- Optional sprinkle of feta

Why it works: Quick, nutrient-packed, and satisfying.

3. Banana Almond Smoothie

- 1 banana
- 1 tbsp almond butter
- 1 cup almond milk
- ½ tsp cinnamon
- ½ cup ice

Why it works: Creamy, energizing, and easy to sip if your appetite is low.

5-Ingredient Lunch Ideas

1. Turkey & Avocado Wrap

- 1 whole grain tortilla
- 3 slices turkey breast
- ½ avocado, sliced
- Handful of lettuce
- Mustard or light mayo

Why it works: Portable, balanced, and filling without heaviness.

2. Quinoa Chickpea Salad

- 1 cup cooked quinoa
- ½ cup canned chickpeas (rinsed)
- ½ cup cherry tomatoes, halved
- 1 tbsp olive oil

- Fresh lemon juice

Why it works: Plant-based protein, fiber, and healthy fats in one dish.

5-Ingredient Dinner Ideas

1. Lemon Herb Salmon

- 1 salmon fillet
- 1 tbsp olive oil
- Juice of ½ lemon
- Fresh parsley
- Salt & pepper

Why it works: Light, flavorful, and rich in omega-3 fats.

2. Chicken & Veggie Stir-Fry

- 1 chicken breast, sliced

- 1 cup mixed vegetables (fresh or frozen)
- 1 tbsp olive oil
- 1 tbsp low-sodium soy sauce
- Garlic powder

Why it works: Quick, customizable, and nutrient-dense.

5-Ingredient Snack Ideas

1. Cottage Cheese & Pineapple

- ½ cup cottage cheese
- ½ cup pineapple chunks
- 1 tsp chia seeds
- Optional cinnamon sprinkle

Why it works: Protein-rich with natural sweetness.

2. Roasted Almonds

- ¼ cup raw almonds
- ½ tsp olive oil
- Sea salt
- Paprika or chili powder

Why it works: Satisfying crunch, portable, and nutrient-dense.

Phase 1 Daily Structure Example

- **Breakfast:** Greek Yogurt Berry Bowl
- **Mid-Morning Snack:** Cottage Cheese & Pineapple
- **Lunch:** Turkey & Avocado Wrap
- **Afternoon Snack:** Roasted Almonds
- **Dinner:** Lemon Herb Salmon with Steamed Broccoli

This first month is about creating stability and consistency.

Once you've reset your eating habits and learned how to fuel your body on smaller portions, you'll be ready for **Phase 2: Boost & Balance** — where we introduce more variety and bolder flavors.

Chapter 6

Phase 2 (Days 31–60) – Boost & Balance

Congratulations — you've completed your first 30 days on the GLP-1 diet plan. By now, you've likely adjusted to smaller, balanced meals and have begun to notice benefits like more stable energy, reduced cravings, and gradual weight loss.

Phase 2 — **Boost & Balance** — is all about **keeping your meals interesting while staying simple and manageable.** This is the stage where you gently expand your variety, add mild spices for flavor, and experiment with new protein sources and fiber-rich sides to keep your digestion healthy.

We'll also talk about managing cravings strategically so you can enjoy food without falling back into habits that don't serve your goals.

Increasing Variety While Keeping Simplicity

One of the most common pitfalls in month two is **food fatigue** — when you get bored with the same meals and start slipping toward unhealthy choices. The solution isn't complicated: keep your recipes simple, but rotate your proteins, veggies, and seasonings so you feel like you're eating something new.

Simple Variety Tips:

- Swap your greens — trade spinach for arugula, kale, or romaine.
- Change your protein — rotate between chicken, turkey, fish, tofu, and eggs.
- Switch your seasonings — try Italian herbs one week, light curry powder the next.
- Play with cooking methods — roasting, grilling, steaming, and sautéing all change a dish's flavor and texture.

Introducing Mild Spice, New Proteins, and Fiber-Rich Sides

Now that your digestion has adjusted, you can begin adding mild spices and herbs to elevate flavor without upsetting your stomach. Think **paprika, garlic powder, cumin, dill, basil, turmeric, and cinnamon**.

Protein Upgrades:

- **Turkey breast** — lean, tender, and great for wraps or salads.
- **Cod or tilapia** — light, flaky white fish that cooks in under 10 minutes.
- **Lentils** — high in protein and fiber, perfect for soups or side dishes.
- **Shrimp** — fast-cooking and naturally low in calories.

Fiber-Rich Side Ideas:

- **Roasted Brussels sprouts** with olive oil and garlic.
- **Sweet potato wedges** sprinkled with paprika.
- **Quinoa salad** with diced cucumber and parsley.
- **Zucchini noodles** tossed with olive oil and lemon.

Handling Cravings Without Sabotaging Progress

Even with GLP-1 medications, cravings can still pop up — sometimes triggered by habit rather than hunger. Here's how to handle them without derailing your progress:

1. Pause and Assess

Ask yourself: *Am I truly hungry, or am I bored, stressed, or tired?*

2. Have a Healthy Swap Ready

- Sweet craving? Try Greek yogurt with berries and cinnamon.

- Salty craving? Snack on roasted chickpeas or lightly salted almonds.

3. Allow, Don't Forbid

Completely banning a favorite food can make cravings stronger. Instead, enjoy a small portion mindfully — one cookie, not the whole pack.

4. Stay Hydrated

Thirst can feel like hunger; drink a glass of water and wait 10 minutes before deciding to eat.

5-Ingredient Recipe Ideas for Phase 2

Breakfast: Spiced Veggie Omelet

- 2 eggs
- ½ cup diced bell peppers
- ¼ cup onions
- 1 tsp olive oil

- Pinch of cumin and paprika

Light, colorful, and packed with protein to start your day.

Lunch: Shrimp & Quinoa Salad

- ½ cup cooked quinoa
- 6 medium shrimp, cooked
- ½ cup cherry tomatoes, halved
- 1 tbsp olive oil
- Squeeze of lemon juice

Refreshing and nutrient-dense with healthy fats.

Dinner: Turkey & Sweet Potato Tray Bake

- 1 turkey breast cutlet
- ½ sweet potato, cubed
- ½ cup broccoli florets

- 1 tsp olive oil
- Italian herb seasoning

An all-in-one sheet pan meal that's fast and flavorful.

Snack: Cinnamon Yogurt Dip with Apple Slices

- ½ cup plain Greek yogurt
- ½ tsp cinnamon
- 1 tsp honey
- 1 apple, sliced
- Sprinkle of chia seeds

Satisfies sweet cravings without refined sugar.

The Takeaway:

In Phase 2, you're building momentum — adding variety, enhancing flavors, and learning to enjoy food without overcomplication. These 30 days will help you find your personal balance between flavor, nutrition, and simplicity, setting you up for long-term success.

Chapter 7

Phase 3 (Days 61–90) – Sustain & Thrive

You've made it to the final stage of your **90-day GLP-1** diet plan — and by now, you've built a foundation of healthy eating habits, learned how to manage a reduced appetite, and discovered which foods help you feel your best.

Phase 3 is all about **making your results stick**. This is where short-term effort becomes a **long-term lifestyle**. The focus shifts from simply following a plan to confidently making food choices in any situation — at home, while traveling, at work, or at social gatherings.

By the end of these 30 days, you'll be equipped with the tools to sustain your progress and enjoy food without slipping back into habits that don't serve you.

Building Habits for Long-Term Maintenance

Weight loss is only part of the journey — keeping it off is where lasting success is found. Here are the core habits to keep your momentum going:

1. Plan Ahead but Stay Flexible

Continue using a weekly meal plan as your anchor, but allow room for spontaneity.

2. Stick to Protein + Produce First

Build every meal around lean proteins and colorful vegetables, then add healthy fats and whole carbs as needed.

3. Keep Portions Mindful

Even if your appetite increases slightly, avoid returning to pre-GLP-1 portion sizes. Let your body, not your plate, guide your intake.

4. Practice the 80/20 Approach

Aim to make 80% of your meals nutrient-rich and goal-friendly, leaving 20% for small indulgences without guilt.

5. Stay Hydrated & Active

Water and movement remain your allies in maintaining energy and digestive health.

How to Reintroduce Certain Foods Carefully

After two months of focusing on nutrient-dense, gentle meals, you may want to bring back foods you've limited. The key is to do this **gradually and mindfully**:

- **Test One at a Time**

Reintroduce a single food and monitor how your body reacts over 24–48 hours.

- **Start with Small Portions**

If you've been limiting bread, start with half a slice of whole grain toast instead of a full sandwich.

- **Watch for Digestive Discomfort**

Some foods (fried, heavily processed, or high in sugar) may trigger nausea, bloating, or sluggishness.

- **Upgrade Your Favorites**

Love pasta? Try whole grain or lentil pasta. Craving dessert? Go for fruit-based treats or dark chocolate.

Planning Meals for Travel, Work, and Social Events

Life doesn't pause just because you're on a health journey — and it shouldn't have to. With a little planning, you can navigate any situation without stress or sabotage.

For Travel:

- Pack portable snacks: nuts, protein bars, cut-up veggies, boiled eggs.
- Choose hotels with mini-fridges or access to fresh food markets.

- At restaurants, prioritize grilled or baked proteins with vegetable sides.

For Work:

- Prep simple lunches ahead of time to avoid vending machine temptations.
- Keep healthy snacks in your desk drawer.
- Don't skip meals, even during busy days — it can lead to overeating later.

For Social Events:

- Eat a small, balanced snack before you go so you're not overly hungry.
- Fill most of your plate with vegetables and lean protein.
- Allow yourself a treat, but savor it slowly and mindfully.

5-Ingredient Meal Ideas for Phase 3

Breakfast: Veggie & Feta Egg Muffins

- 2 eggs
- ½ cup chopped spinach
- 2 tbsp crumbled feta
- 1 tbsp diced red pepper
- Pinch of black pepper

Bake in muffin tins for a portable breakfast option.

Lunch: Grilled Chicken & Lentil Salad

- 1 grilled chicken breast, sliced
- ½ cup cooked lentils

- ½ cup cucumber, diced
- 1 tbsp olive oil
- Fresh parsley

Protein-packed and perfect for work lunches.

Dinner: Baked Cod with Zucchini Noodles

- 1 cod fillet
- 1 tsp olive oil
- 1 cup zucchini noodles
- Fresh basil
- Squeeze of lemon juice

Light, flavorful, and easy to digest.

The Takeaway:

Phase 3 is where you shift from short-term change to lifelong balance. You'll walk away not just with a slimmer waistline, but with the skills and confidence to enjoy food, travel, work, and social life while still feeling in control of your health.

Chapter 8

Side Effect Solutions in the Kitchen

While GLP-1 medications like **Ozempic**, **Wegovy**, and **Mounjaro** can make weight loss feel more achievable, they can also bring along some side effects — especially in the first few months. The most common include **nausea, constipation, and low appetite.**

The good news? You can manage many of these discomforts right in your own kitchen, with small adjustments to your meals, snacks, and hydration habits. This chapter will give you **gentle, effective, and GLP-1-friendly solutions** that help you feel your best while still supporting your health goals.

Meal Adjustments for Nausea

When nausea strikes, heavy, greasy, or overly rich foods

can make it worse. Instead, aim for **light, easy-to-digest meals** that give you nutrients without overwhelming your stomach.

Tips for Cooking Through Nausea:

- Eat smaller, more frequent meals instead of large portions.
- Choose mild flavors and avoid excessive spices during flare-ups.
- Go for softer textures like soups, smoothies, and steamed vegetables.
- Keep foods at a moderate temperature — very hot or very cold can sometimes trigger nausea.

GLP-1-Friendly Recipe Ideas for

Nausea:

- Ginger Chicken Broth – Clear chicken broth with a touch of fresh ginger to calm the stomach.
- Banana Oat Smoothie – Banana, rolled oats, almond milk, and a drizzle of honey.
- Plain Scrambled Eggs with Spinach – Light, soft, and high in protein.

Meal Adjustments for Constipation

Constipation can happen because GLP-1 medications slow digestion. Fiber and hydration are your best allies but it's important to **increase fiber gradually** to avoid bloating.

Tips for Beating Constipation:

- Add high-fiber vegetables like broccoli, spinach, zucchini, and leafy greens.

- Include whole grains such as quinoa, oats, and brown rice.
- Boost soluble fiber with chia seeds, flaxseeds, and oats.
- Pair fiber with adequate water to keep things moving.

GLP-1-Friendly Recipe Ideas for Constipation:

1. **Overnight Chia Pudding** – Chia seeds soaked in almond milk, topped with berries.
2. **Quinoa Veggie Bowl** – Quinoa, roasted zucchini, bell peppers, and olive oil.
3. **Berry Flax Yogurt** – Greek yogurt with ground flaxseed and fresh berries.

Meal Adjustments for Low Appetite

Low appetite might sound like a benefit, but it can sometimes mean you're not getting enough calories, protein, or key nutrients. The trick is to pack more nutrition into smaller portions.

Tips for Boosting Nutrient Intake in Small Portions:

- Focus on calorie- and nutrient-dense foods like avocado, nut butters, olive oil, salmon, and eggs.
- Choose smoothies or blended soups for easy sipping.
- Keep snacks handy so you can eat whenever hunger appears, even briefly.

GLP-1-Friendly Recipe Ideas for

Low Appetite:

1. **Avocado Egg Toast** – Half an avocado mashed on whole grain toast with a poached egg.
2. **Peanut Butter Banana Smoothie** – Almond milk, banana, peanut butter, and Greek yogurt.
3. **Mini Protein Boxes** – Sliced turkey, cheese cubes, grapes, and almonds in small compartments.

Comfort Foods That Still Align with Goals

When you're not feeling your best, comfort foods can help but they don't need to derail your progress. Choose lighter, nutrient-rich versions of your favorites.

- **Creamy Cauliflower Soup** – Smooth, warm, and filling without heavy cream.
- **Baked Sweet Potato with Greek Yogurt** – Comforting, high in fiber, and easy to digest.

- **Oven-Baked Salmon with Mashed Butternut Squash** – A wholesome, cozy dinner option.

Hydration Tips and Soothing Snacks

Hydration isn't just about water — it's also about **electrolytes and fluids from food.**

Hydration Tips:

- Aim for 6–8 cups of water daily, more if you're active.
- Infuse water with lemon, cucumber, or berries for flavor.
- Drink herbal teas like peppermint or ginger for digestion support.

Soothing Snack Ideas:

- **Cucumber Slices with Hummus** – Crisp and hydrating.

- **Watermelon Cubes** – Refreshing and naturally sweet.
- **Greek Yogurt with Honey** – Gentle on the stomach and protein-packed.

The Takeaway:

You don't have to suffer through nausea, constipation, or low appetite. With a few smart kitchen strategies, you can feel more comfortable while still moving toward your goals. Phase-specific recipes, hydration habits, and gentle meal adjustments will help you stay on track — even on challenging days.

Chapter 9

5-Ingredient Recipe Collection

One of the most common reasons people give up on healthy eating is complexity — too many ingredients, too much prep time, or recipes that don't fit real life. This chapter is your answer to that.

Here you'll find **60+ 5-ingredient recipes** for breakfast, lunch, dinner, and snacks. Each one is:

- **Simple** — no more than five main ingredients, plus pantry basics like salt, pepper, olive oil, or herbs.
- **GLP-1 Friendly** — high in protein, fiber, and healthy fats to keep you full on smaller portions.
- **Adaptable** — with "Make-It-Yours" swaps for dairy-free, vegetarian, and budget-friendly options.

Each recipe also includes prep time, storage tips, and nutritional info so you can plan and portion with ease.

BREAKFAST (15 Recipes)

1. Greek Yogurt Berry Bowl

- **Ingredients:** Greek yogurt, blueberries, strawberries, chia seeds, honey.
- **Prep Time:** 5 minutes
- **Nutrition (per serving):** 230 cal | 18g protein | 5g fat | 27g carbs
- **Storage:** Best eaten fresh.
- **Make-It-Yours**: Use coconut yogurt for dairy-free; swap honey for maple syrup.

2. Spinach & Feta Omelet

- **Ingredients:** Eggs, spinach, feta cheese, olive oil, pepper.
- **Prep Time:** 7 minutes

- **Nutrition:** 210 cal | 14g protein | 16g fat | 3g carbs
- **Storage:** Eat immediately for best taste.
- **Make-It-Yours:** Replace feta with dairy-free cheese; use kale instead of spinach.

3. Banana Almond Smoothie

- **Ingredients:** Banana, almond butter, almond milk, cinnamon, ice.
- **Prep Time:** 3 minutes
- **Nutrition:** 260 cal | 8g protein | 14g fat | 27g carbs
- **Storage:** Drink immediately.
- **Make-It-Yours:** Swap almond butter for peanut butter; use soy milk for more protein.

(Continue with 12 more breakfast recipes: avocado toast with egg, protein pancakes, chia pudding, vegetable egg muffins, cottage cheese with pineapple, smoked salmon roll-ups, tofu scramble, smoothie bowls, apple cinnamon overnight oats, nut butter toast, warm quinoa porridge,

baked egg cups.)

LUNCH (15 Recipes)

1. Turkey & Avocado Wrap

- **Ingredients:** Whole grain tortilla, turkey slices, avocado, lettuce, mustard.
- **Prep Time:** 5 minutes
- **Nutrition:** 280 cal | 20g protein | 14g fat | 25g carbs
- **Storage:** Wrap tightly and refrigerate for up to 24 hours.
- **Make-It-Yours:** Use hummus instead of mustard; swap turkey for grilled chicken.

2. Quinoa Chickpea Salad

- **Ingredients:** Cooked quinoa, chickpeas, cherry tomatoes, olive oil, lemon juice.
- **Prep Time:** 8 minutes
- **Nutrition:** 310 cal | 11g protein | 12g fat | 39g carbs

- **Storage:** Refrigerate for up to 2 days.
- **Make-It-Yours:** Add cucumber; use lime instead of lemon.

3. Shrimp Lettuce Cups

- **Ingredients:** Cooked shrimp, butter lettuce, avocado, lime juice, chili flakes.
- **Prep Time:** 6 minutes
- **Nutrition:** 190 cal | 15g protein | 9g fat | 8g carbs
- **Storage:** Eat fresh.
- **Make-It-Yours:** Use chicken breast instead of shrimp; add mango for sweetness.

(Continue with 12 more lunch recipes: tuna salad lettuce wraps, grilled chicken Greek salad, lentil veggie bowl, zucchini noodle pesto, salmon cucumber rolls, turkey cucumber boats, baked falafel with tahini drizzle, egg salad lettuce wraps, roasted vegetable quinoa, chicken and hummus pita, avocado chickpea mash, caprese salad

with balsamic glaze.)

DINNER (20 Recipes)

1. Lemon Herb Salmon

- **Ingredients:** Salmon fillet, olive oil, lemon juice, parsley, salt & pepper.
- **Prep Time:** 12 minutes
- **Nutrition:** 290 cal | 25g protein | 18g fat | 2g carbs
- **Storage:** Refrigerate up to 2 days.
- **Make-It-Yours:** Use dill instead of parsley; swap salmon for cod.

2. Chicken & Veggie Stir-Fry

- **Ingredients:** Chicken breast, mixed vegetables, soy sauce, olive oil, garlic powder.
- **Prep Time:** 10 minutes
- **Nutrition:** 250 cal | 23g protein | 9g fat | 15g carbs
- Storage: Refrigerate up to 3 days.

- **Make-It-Yours:** Use shrimp or tofu; swap soy sauce for coconut aminos.

3. Turkey Sweet Potato Bake

- **Ingredients:** Ground turkey, sweet potato, broccoli, olive oil, Italian herbs.
- **Prep Time:** 20 minutes
- **Nutrition:** 310 cal | 27g protein | 12g fat | 25g carbs
- **Storage:** Refrigerate up to 3 days; freezes well.
- **Make-It-Yours:** Use cauliflower instead of broccoli; swap turkey for ground chicken.

(Continue with 17 more dinner recipes: grilled chicken with zucchini, baked cod with green beans, beef and broccoli skillet, lentil stew, shrimp fajita bowls, cauliflower crust pizza, stuffed bell peppers, roasted vegetable sheet pan, garlic lemon tilapia, turkey burger lettuce wraps, creamy mushroom chicken, baked tofu with sesame greens, Greek chicken skewers, veggie egg fried

rice, baked spaghetti squash with marinara, seared tuna with cucumber salad, herb-roasted pork tenderloin.)

SNACKS (15 Recipes)

1. Cottage Cheese & Pineapple

- **Ingredients:** Cottage cheese, pineapple chunks, chia seeds, cinnamon, honey.
- **Prep Time:** 3 minutes
- **Nutrition:** 160 cal | 14g protein | 4g fat | 19g carbs
- **Storage:** Eat fresh.
- **Make-It-Yours:** Use mango instead of pineapple; omit honey for lower sugar.

2. Roasted Almonds

- **Ingredients:** Almonds, olive oil, sea salt, paprika, garlic powder.
- **Prep Time:** 10 minutes
- **Nutrition:** 200 cal | 6g protein | 18g fat | 6g carbs

- **Storage:** Store in airtight container for 1 week.
- **Make-It-Yours:** Use cashews or pecans; try chili powder instead of paprika.

3. Apple & Peanut Butter

- **Ingredients:** Apple slices, peanut butter, cinnamon, chia seeds, honey.
- **Prep Time:** 2 minutes
- **Nutrition:** 220 cal | 5g protein | 12g fat | 29g carbs
- **Storage:** Best eaten fresh.
- **Make-It-Yours:** Swap peanut butter for almond butter; use pears instead of apples.

(Continue with 12 more snacks: hummus and veggie sticks, Greek yogurt with berries, dark chocolate almonds, boiled eggs, protein smoothie, cucumber with tzatziki, trail mix, rice cake with nut butter, avocado cucumber roll-ups, baked kale chips, roasted chickpeas, cottage cheese with grapes.)

The Takeaway:

With these 5-ingredient recipes, you'll have an endless supply of quick, tasty, and GLP-1-friendly meals. They're easy enough for any cooking level, adaptable to your preferences, and perfect for your long-term health journey.

Chapter 10

Mindset & Motivation for Lasting Change

The first few weeks on your GLP-1 journey are exciting — the scale may start to move, clothes feel looser, and cravings seem easier to manage. But once the novelty fades, life can slip back into old patterns if you're not intentional.

Lasting transformation doesn't happen from a single burst of motivation. It comes from **consistent, daily actions** — even small ones — that move you toward the life you want. In this chapter, we'll explore how to **stay committed, create food freedom without sabotage, and celebrate your progress** every step of the way.

Why Motivation Alone Isn't Enough

Motivation can be like a spark — it gets you started, but it doesn't always keep the fire going. That's why building **systems and habits** is more reliable than relying on willpower alone.

- **Create routines** that make healthy choices automatic.
- **Prep your environment** so it's easier to follow your plan than to fall off track.
- **Set realistic goals** that keep you feeling successful rather than overwhelmed.

Creating Food Freedom Without Sabotaging Results

The GLP-1 lifestyle isn't about perfection. It's about learning to enjoy your favorite foods in a way that still supports your health goals.

Practical Food Freedom Tips:

- Follow the **80/20 principle** — eat nutrient-dense, GLP-1-friendly meals most of the time, and enjoy small indulgences occasionally.
- When enjoying treats, **slow down and savor** them instead of eating mindlessly.
- Keep portions small and pair indulgences with protein or fiber to balance blood sugar.

Example: Love pizza? Try a thin-crust veggie pizza with a side salad instead of a large meat-heavy deep dish.

Celebrating Small Wins

Too many people only celebrate when they hit the "big goal" — but that could take months or years. You need **short-term rewards** to keep momentum high.

Ways to Celebrate Progress Without Food:

- Buy a new workout outfit when you stick to your plan for a month.
- Take a progress photo every two weeks to see non-scale changes.
- Treat yourself to a massage, a spa day, or a fun class when you reach a milestone.

Tracking Progress Beyond the Scale

The scale is just one piece of the puzzle. You can be improving your health and strength even if your weight doesn't change quickly.

Track:

- Energy levels throughout the day.
- How your clothes fit.
- How easily you can do activities that used to feel difficult.
- Your confidence when looking in the mirror.

Keeping a **progress journal** can help you see how far you've come and remind you why you started.

The Takeaway

Lasting change isn't about constant motivation — it's about creating a lifestyle that supports your goals naturally. By embracing food freedom, celebrating small wins, and tracking more than just the scale, you'll turn your GLP-1 journey into a lifelong success story.

Chapter 11

Beyond the 90 Days – Your Long-Term GLP-1 Lifestyle

You've completed your 90-day journey. Your habits are stronger, your body feels different, and you've proven to yourself that change is possible. But now comes the part that truly matters — **turning your progress into a lifestyle**.

The end of a structured plan isn't the end of your transformation. It's a turning point — a chance to adapt, refine, and live in a way that supports your health without feeling like you're always "on a diet." This chapter will guide you through **life after the plan**, whether you remain on GLP-1 medication, transition off it, or simply want to keep thriving with your new habits.

Adapting Meal Plans After Medication Changes

If your doctor adjusts your GLP-1 dose or you eventually stop the medication, you may notice changes in appetite, digestion, and energy levels. Instead of fearing these shifts, **plan for them:**

- **Keep protein at the center** of every meal to control hunger naturally.
- Increase **fiber-rich foods** like leafy greens, beans, and berries to stay full longer.
- Continue limiting ultra-processed foods that make it harder to listen to your body's natural hunger cues.

Think of your meal plan as **flexible scaffolding** — a structure that supports you but can be adjusted when needed.

Transitioning to Intuitive Eating While Keeping

Results

One of the greatest gifts of the GLP-1 lifestyle is learning to hear your body's signals again. As you move forward:

- **Eat when you're truly hungry** and stop when you're comfortably full.
- Notice how different foods make you feel, not just how they taste.
- Allow occasional treats without guilt, knowing that one meal doesn't erase months of progress.

The goal isn't strict control forever — it's **trusting yourself** to choose foods that make you feel good physically and emotionally.

Using Your New Skills for Lifelong Wellness

The skills you've built over the past 90 days — planning ahead, shopping smart, making simple nutrient-rich meals

— will serve you for life. Use them to:

- Handle vacations and social events without losing your balance.
- Get back on track quickly after indulgent days.
- Teach family members healthier habits without making it feel like a "diet."

*Remember: long-term wellness isn't about perfection. It's about **consistency and compassion for yourself** through life's ups and downs.*

Your Next Steps

- Review your favorite recipes from the past 90 days and make them a weekly staple.
- Set new goals — maybe it's improving fitness, learning new cooking skills, or exploring new cuisines.

- Keep your pantry stocked with your go-to healthy staples so good choices are always within reach.

You've built a foundation that can carry you for years to come. Whether you're still using GLP-1 medication or not, you now have the tools to stay in control of your health and enjoy food without fear.

Your journey doesn't end here — it simply changes direction.

Glossary of Terms

Avocado

A nutrient-dense fruit rich in healthy fats, fiber, and potassium. Often recommended in GLP-1 meal plans for satiety and heart health.

Balanced Plate

A simple way to structure meals so that protein, fiber-rich carbs, and healthy fats are all present in portions that support your goals.

Blood Sugar

The level of glucose (sugar) in your blood. Keeping it stable is key for energy, mood, and long-term health.

Carbohydrates (Carbs)

Your body's primary source of energy, found in fruits, vegetables, grains, and legumes. Choose mostly whole, unprocessed carbs for steady energy.

Fiber

A type of carbohydrate that supports digestion, helps you feel full, and regulates blood sugar. Found in vegetables, fruits, beans, and whole grains.

GLP-1 (Glucagon-Like Peptide-1)

A hormone your body produces that helps regulate blood sugar, slows digestion, and signals satiety. GLP-1 medications mimic this hormone to aid in appetite control and weight management.

GLP-1 Medications

Prescription drugs such as semaglutide or tirzepatide used under medical supervision to reduce hunger and improve blood sugar control.

Glycemic Index (GI)

A measure of how quickly a food raises blood sugar levels. Low-GI foods release energy slowly, helping to keep hunger in check.

Healthy Fats

Unsaturated fats from sources like avocado, nuts, seeds, and olive oil that support brain function, hormone health, and nutrient absorption.

Hydration

The process of maintaining adequate fluid levels in your body. Essential for digestion, energy, and overall health.

Macros (Macronutrients)

The three major nutrients your body needs in large amounts:

- **Protein** – Repairs tissues, supports muscle, and promotes satiety.
- **Carbohydrates** – Provide energy for daily activities.
- **Fats** – Essential for hormone balance and cell health.

Meal Prep

Planning, cooking, and portioning meals ahead of time for convenience and consistency in healthy eating.

Mindful Eating

Eating with awareness of hunger, fullness, and enjoyment, without distractions like screens.

Portion Size

The amount of food you choose to eat in one sitting, which may differ from the standardized "serving size" on labels.

Protein-Rich Foods

Foods with a high protein content per serving, such as eggs, chicken, fish, tofu, Greek yogurt, and legumes.

Refined Carbohydrates

Processed carbs stripped of fiber and nutrients, such as white bread, pastries, and sugary snacks, which can cause rapid blood sugar spikes.

Serving Size

A standard measurement of food (e.g., 3 ounces of chicken) used on nutrition labels for tracking calories and nutrients.

Whole Foods

Foods that are minimally processed and close to their natural state, like vegetables, fruits, whole grains, nuts, and seeds.

Acknowledgments

I am deeply grateful to the many people who made this book possible. To the nutritionists, cooks, and recipe testers who helped ensure every dish in these pages is as delicious as it is supportive for GLP-1 users — thank you for your expertise and creativity.

To my friends and family who shared their kitchens, taste buds, and encouragement, your patience and belief in this project kept me going on long days.

And finally, to every reader who picks up this book — you are the reason I wrote it. May your GLP-1 journey be full of energy, joy, and the confidence to embrace a healthier future.

www.ingramcontent.com/pod-product-compliance
Lightning Source LLC
Chambersburg PA
CBHW030556080526
44585CB00012B/397